Young Strings in Action

A String Method for Class or Individual Instruction

PAUL ROLLAND'S
Approach to String Playing

Compiled and Edited by
SHEILA JOHNSON

STUDENT BOOK
Viola

Music Arranged by
Robert Wharton

DISTRIBUTED BY
HAL•LEONARD® CORPORATION
7777 W. BLUEMOUND RD. P.O. BOX 13819 MILWAUKEE, WI 53213

CONTENTS

Cassette tapes containing the exercises and teaching pieces featured in this publication
are available on sale

*Young musicians are encouraged to use the tapes to promote ear-training
and improve overall musicianship.*

THE ROLLAND PHILOSOPHY

"Get them started right and aim them in the right direction and they will reach the top . . . . It is a fallacy to believe that the careful teaching of fundamentals will slow down the pupil . . . . Most elements of string playing can be introduced, in embryonic form of course, during the first year of instruction, and refined thereafter . . . . One would be quite surprised at what pupils can be started on during the first and second years . . . . Music educators should strive to develop players who not only play in tune with a good sound but who also feel comfortable and happy in so doing, and who use well coordinated movements without excessive tension as they play . . . . It is of paramount importance to develop a well balanced stance, balanced right and left arms, and a balanced hold . . . . Good balance is the key to efficient movements . . . . A small child can be taught to play with a beautiful tone and sonority by the use of good balance of the body and by avoiding static tensions in his movements . . . . Stressed is freedom of movement: trying to inculcate the pupil with a feeling of kinesthesia, a feeling of lightness, both with the bow and the instrument . . . . naturalness, naturalness, naturalness . . . ."

— Paul Rolland

ENDORSEMENTS

No one has rendered greater service to violin playing than Paul Rolland. Of that rare breed of men of a mind as penetrating as it is open, he brought to our special art a talent and dedication which could as easily have made sense and brought order to issues of more universal and widespread chaos — the conservation of energy, distribution of resources, economy of communication techniques, for instance, to name but a few! He chose the violin and bow, concentrating on the workings of ten fingers in a very limited area, in their myriad functions of support and expression, transmitting the impulses of body, mind and heart, and receiving, as antennae, the soul waves of humanity at large.

He has organically absorbed the best of Suzuki, for instance (not simply grafted, but integrated), and by bringing his original mind to bear on teaching, bequeathed us what is one of the very best books on violin playing and teaching, as well as films of enormous value.

In recognizing his contribution, we can save years of blind confusing effort and money — for what is a great man's gift other than to point the way and save humanity heartache and wasting drift.

> — Yehudi Menuhin

Paul Rolland's contributions to string playing and teaching have been historically significant. **Prelude to String Playing** *or now* **Young Strings in Action** *is a major part of his contribution. I hope and suggest its widespread use.*

> — Janos Starker — Cellist
> Distinguished Professor
> Indiana University, Music
> Bloomington, Indiana

I am honored to express my views on **Young Strings in Action,** *the Rolland string teaching method, revised by Sheila Johnson.*

You have in Paul Rolland, a genius in string pedagogy. His extensive research, thought, and application show him to be years ahead of his time, and surely comparable with the finest teachers in violin history. His attention to balance, efficiency of movement, relaxation, and posture show great insight into the disciplines of kinesiology and science. His methods result in an ease in playing, and a tastefully musical quality in young performers.

The literature Sheila Johnson has included and augmented from the original work is clearly presented, accurate, and reveals the exuberant, upbeat character that marked the teaching of Paul Rolland, and today, Sheila Johnson. Paul Rolland often skipped, danced, and smiled as he played or taught — learning was indeed great fun.

Mr. Rolland was keenly interested in his private teaching and research before he began the writing of this original material. His concern for the public school music grew as he saw a tremendous need to aid in mass string teaching at a high level. It seems to me most commendable that from a comfortable private teaching situation at the University of Illinois, he was willing to identify the need and systematically present his method, thus becoming a part of the solution of teaching the young string player.

His methods, vocabulary, and charming approach to string playing work! For over twenty years I have been able to successfully reproduce string players and bow arms which prompted him before his untimely death to call these students "my grandchildren."

Young Strings in Action *is the ultimate legacy of Paul Rolland, revised by a favorite pupil of his — Sheila Johnson. CAUTION! Its use could revolutionize string playing the world over!!*

> — Susan S. Starrett
> No. Aurora, Illinois

I am very excited to see this volume. I have admired the work which Paul Rolland has done for string teaching, and although his writing and films have proved very helpful, Sheila Johnson's reorganization of the teaching materials in a format that can be used to plan the development of a program from the beginning on in sequence is a great achievement. This is surely a work of love, devotion, and expertise.

> — Dr. Kenneth Sarch, Professor of Violin
> Shenandoah Conservatory of Music
> Winchester, Virginia

Mr. Rolland has called upon a lifetime of experience as performer and teacher in producing this important work. In simple, clear language it systematically takes up the elements of string technique in detail. Excellent drawings, diagrams and photographs accompany and illustrate the text. Both remedial and developmental techniques are included. Mr. Rolland has thoroughly studied and mastered the rich pedagogical tradition from which contemporary string teaching has evolved, and he draws upon the experience and wisdom of many of its articulate pedagogs in support of its principles, principles which urge and guide us toward the discovery of an involved "use of the self" with all that this brings in the way of improved string technique. As a teaching manual, **Young Strings in Action** *is certain to command wide acceptance and use by string teachers everywhere.*

– Francis Tursi, Professor of Viola
Eastman School of Music
Rochester, New York

Paul Rolland devoted his life to improving the quality of string teaching and playing. His inventive genius never stopped working towards this goal. He sought to inspire string teachers to be innovate and open-minded. Since his untimely death Sheila Johnson, one of his most able students, with her dynamic, charismatic personality has helped to establish a most successful Rolland trend among young string players in the U.S. and abroad.

Ms. Johnson has now revised **Prelude to String Playing** *in true Rolland tradition. Paul Rolland would justly be proud of the work which she, with her innovative talents, has carried out most competently. I am glad to have this opportunity to endorse the work Sheila Johnson has done so excellently. String teachers will find* **Young Strings in Action** *the most exciting and inspirational material available to string students.*

– Clara Rolland

ACKNOWLEDGEMENTS

Photographs by Mimi Levine

A special 'Thank You' to **Mrs. Clara Rolland,** *for her encouragement, help and support, and to all who contributed to this revision.*

Sheila Johnson
January, 1985

TERMINOLOGY OF INSTRUMENTS AND BOWS

VIOLA

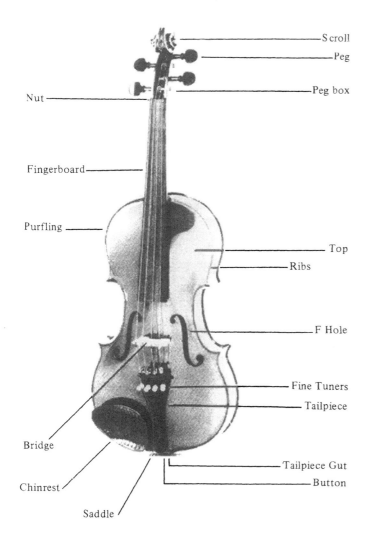
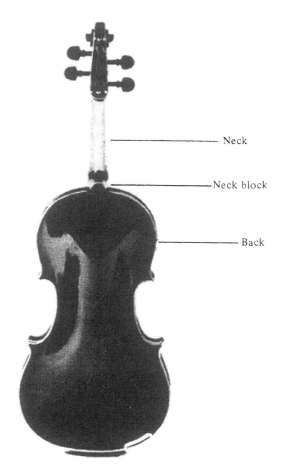

Scroll

Peg

Peg box

Nut

Neck

Fingerboard

Neck block

Purfling

Back

Top

Ribs

F Hole

Fine Tuners

Tailpiece

Bridge

Tailpiece Gut

Button

Chinrest

Saddle

VIOLA BOW

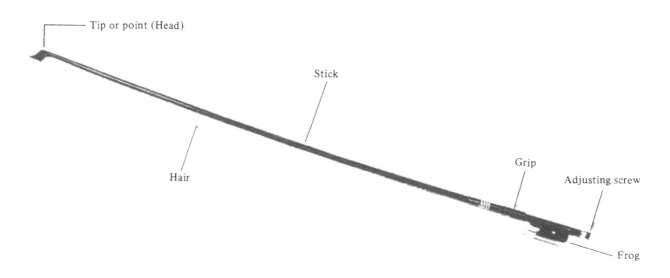

Tip or point (Head)

Stick

Grip

Adjusting screw

Hair

Frog

CARE AND MAINTENANCE OF THE INSTRUMENT

1. Always keep the instrument and bow in the case when not in use, to avoid damage.

2. Do not stuff music into the instrument case.

3. Make a habit of closing the locks on the case even when it is empty.

4. After each playing session, wipe off all rosin dust from the instrument, strings and bow stick, but not the hair. A *clean, dry* soft cloth should be used, with no cleaning agents.

5. When placing the bow in the case, make sure the hair is loosened so that the tension is removed from the arch of the stick. Similarly, when preparing to use the bow, make sure not to tighten the hair too much; it should never be so tight that the bow's inward arch is entirely eliminated.

6. String adjusters should not be turned all the way down so that they scratch the top of the instrument.

7. If pegs are slipping, they may be treated with a commercial "peg dope," by a competent repair person. *Never* use chalk or any other abrasive.

8. Adjustment screws on tuners may be lubricated with a light machine oil, used *very* sparingly.

9. The bridge should be tilted slightly back toward the tailpiece. It is kept in position by the pressure of the strings. Under *no* circumstances should it ever be glued to the top. (In fact, *nothing* should ever be glued except by an expert.)

   The *high* side of the bridge is under the C string.

10. Storage: A great deal of unnecessary repair work results from improper storage. Keep instrument out of excessively dry or damp areas and away from radiators and hot air vents. An ideal temperature is about 70 degrees Fahrenheit, with a relative humidity of 45-50%. (In other words, what feels most comfortable for you is also best for your string instrument.)

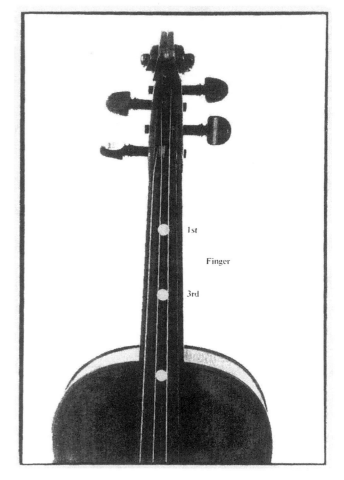

NOTE ON TUNING

The four strings of the viola are tuned, from left to right, C, G, D and A:

In the early stages tuning is mainly the responsibility of the teacher. Listen carefully as the teacher helps you tune your instrument and see if you can tell whether the note is "just right," or too low or too high.

ACTION 1
ESTABLISHING CORRECT PLACEMENT OF THE INSTRUMENT

POSITIONING THE FEET

1. Make a "V" with the heels together.

2. Step a little to the left and shift weight toward left foot. Balance.

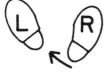

4. STATUE OF LIBERTY

3. REST POSITION

5. PLAYING POSITION

ACTION 2
THE SHUTTLE BETWEEN REGISTERS (The Shuttle Game)

Shuttle with comfortable and unhurried motions.

Step One

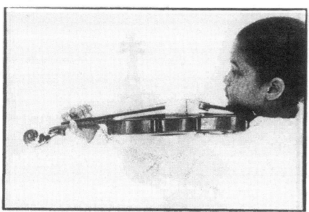

The left hand is in the LOW REGISTER
(1st or 2nd position)

Step Three

The left hand is in the HIGH REGISTER
(6th position and above). The thumb should not
be wrapped around the throat of the neck!

Step Two

The left hand is in the MIDDLE REGISTER
(3rd, 4th, 5th positions)

CASE WALK
Remove instruments and bows
from cases, and close locks.

THREE OPEN STRING TUNES

1.

Johnson

Pluck with the left pinkie

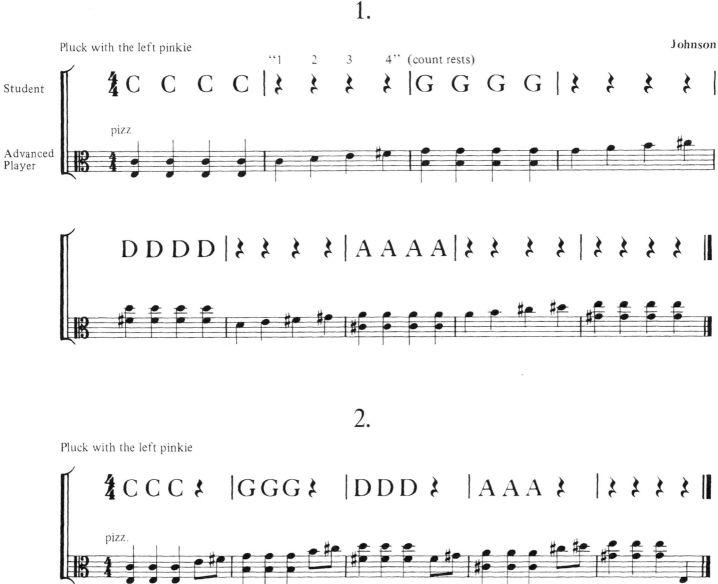

2.

Pluck with the left pinkie

3.

Pluck with the left pinkie

ACTION 3
MOVING ACROSS THE STRINGS

PLUCKED OPEN STRING ACCOMPANIMENTS

Play these tunes with slight movement of the elbow to promote relaxation in the left arm shoulder joint.

4. LIGHTLY ROW

5. CAMPTOWN RACES

STEPHEN COLLINS FOSTER
(1826–1864)

6. HOT CROSS BUNS

Pluck with the left pinkie

7. SKIP TO MY LOU

Pluck with the left pinkie

8. LET US CHASE THE SQUIRREL

Pluck with the left pinkie

Traditional

9. JINGLE BELLS

Pluck with the left pinkie

ACTION 4
LEARNING TO HOLD THE BOW

Step One

Balance the bow on the upper right corner of the thumb tip.

Step Two

The second and third finger embrace the far side of the bow.

Step Three

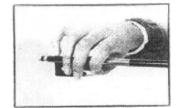

The bow hold is not too tight, not too loose. The fingers are curved.

EXERCISES TO DEVELOP FINGER FLEXIBILITY

Using a pencil or a dowel stick, form a circle by making an "O" with the thumb and second (middle) finger. Slide the pencil between the tip of the bent thumb and the first crease of the second finger. Make sure your fingers are curved and relaxed. Tap the little finger.

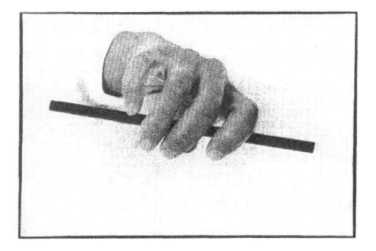

SPIDER CRAWL: With the bow pointing up, "crawl" with the fingertips from the frog to the tip and back down to the frog again (lowering and raising the bow in the air).

WINDSHIELD WIPER: With the proper bow hold, rotate the bow from left to right. Do not let the fingers wrap around the stick. Notice the pressure on the third and fourth fingers.

STIR THE POT: Hold the frog with the fingers, aiming the bow tip up, with the frog pointing to the floor. Move the bow in circles as if stirring a large pot of soup.

ACTION 5
SHADOW BOWING

With the left hand place the tube on the left shoulder. Move the bow through the tube.

Hold the tube out in front of the body with the thumb facing the body.

ACTION 6
HOLDING INSTRUMENT AND BOW TOGETHER

Hold the instrument in playing position with the left hand covering the signal dot, pinkie outstretched. With the right hand, grasp the bow at the balance point, using the "correct bow hold" and hook the tip of the bow over the outstretched left pinkie. Slide the right hand down to the frog. Practice raising and lowering the bow with the right hand.

ACTION 7
SITTING POSITION

When playing in sitting position, always use an armless straight chair.

ACTION 8
RELAXING THE SHOULDER

Set the bow on the bridge, and silently cross from the highest to the lowest string and back with easy, relaxed movements. Do this repeatedly in different parts of the bow as directed by the teacher.

ACTION 9
SHORT STROKES AT THE MIDDLE OF THE BOW

BOWING SYMBOLS:

⊓   V   ,

This is a Down-Bow sign   This is an Up-Bow sign   Lift bow or stop bow:
(move bow to the right)   (move bow to the left)

10.

Rolland

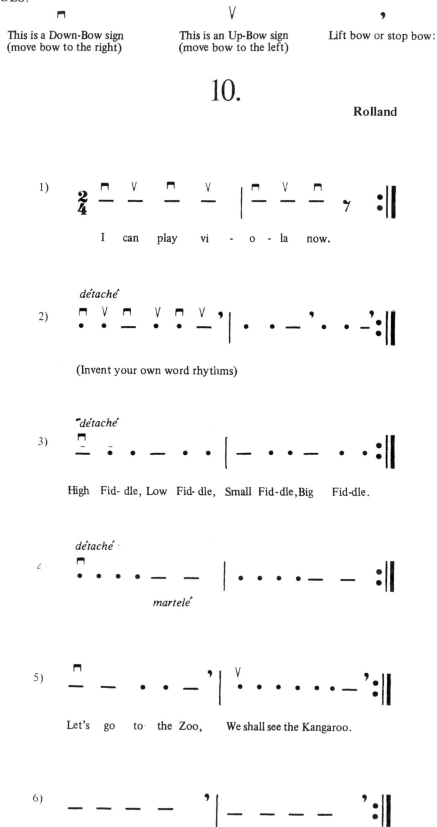

1) I can play vi - o - la now.

2) *détaché*

(Invent your own word rhythms)

3) *détaché*

High Fid- dle, Low Fid- dle, Small Fid-dle, Big Fid-dle.

4) *détaché*

martelé

5) Let's go to the Zoo, We shall see the Kangaroo.

6)

ACTION 10
PLAYING OPEN STRING ACCOMPANIMENTS USING THE BOW

11. LIGHTLY ROW

12. CAMPTOWN RACES

FOSTER

13. HOT CROSS BUNS

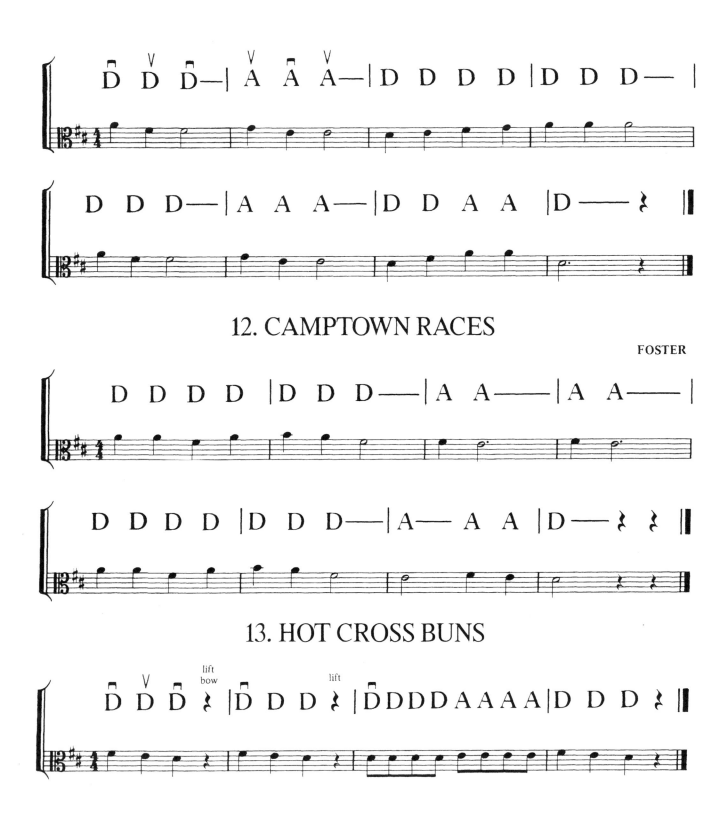

14. SKIP TO MY LOU WITH VARIATIONS

Variation I

Variation II

15. LET US CHASE THE SQUIRREL

Traditional

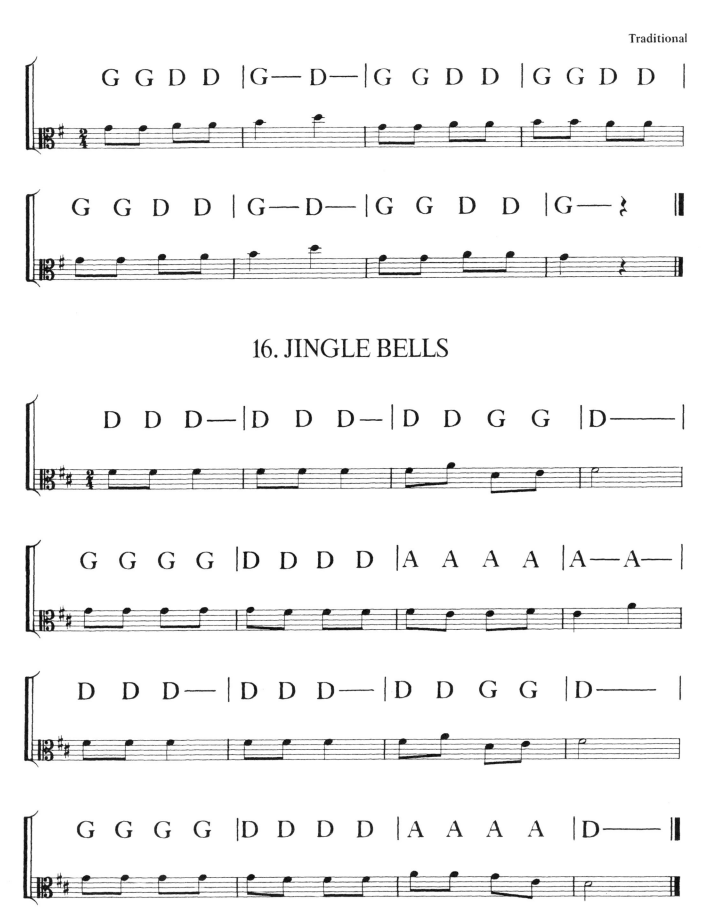

16. JINGLE BELLS

13

NOTE-READING

This is the musical STAFF. It has five lines and four spaces.

the five lines   the four spaces

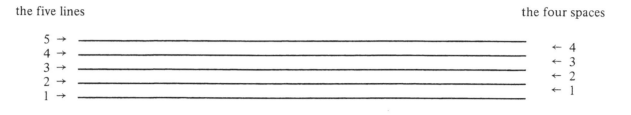

```
5 →  _____    ← 4
4 →  _____    ← 3
3 →  _____    ← 2
2 →  _____    ← 1
1 →  _____
```

Additional lines and spaces can be created by adding LEDGER LINES above and below the staff.

```
ledger lines   3rd →  ___   ← 4th   spaces above staff
above staff    2nd →  ___   ← 3rd
               1st →  ___   ← 2nd
                            ← 1st
```

```
               ledger lines   1st →  ___   ← 1st   spaces
               below staff                ← 2nd    below staff
```

The notes are named after the first seven letters of the alphabet: A, B, C, D, E, F and G. Notes can be written right on the lines or in the spaces. These examples show how notes are written on the staff. We will learn to read these notes during the Actions to follow.

NOTES WRITTEN ON LINES

NOTES WRITTEN IN SPACES

NOTES WRITTEN ON LINES AND IN SPACES

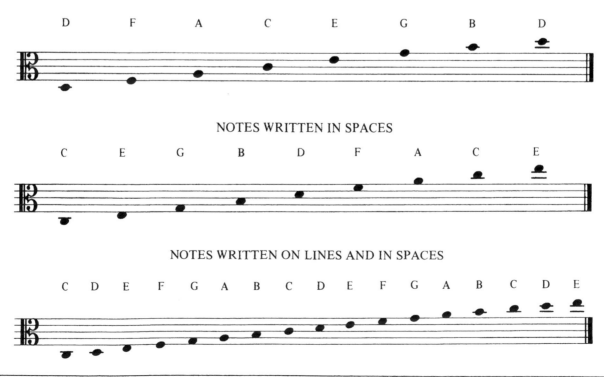

KEY SIGNATURES AND ACCIDENTALS

Sharp: #   Raises the note a half step.

Flat: ♭   Lowers the note a half step.

Natural: ♮   Lowers a sharp note, or raises a flat note a half step.

↑

Alto Clef

Key Signatures:
One or more sharps or flats next to the clef indicate that those notes are always sharp or flat throughout the staff, unless altered by accidentals.

Accidentals:
A sharp or flat (or natural) which is not in the key signature, but which is placed before a note, is called an accidental. An accidental alters the pitch of its note, and all repetitions of that note within the same measure, unless it is cancelled by another accidental.

RHYTHM

Barlines and Measures: Barlines divide the music into equal measures.

↓   Barlines   ↓   Double Bar ↓

↑   Measures   ↑   (the end)

 Time Signature:
This is the signature for "four quarter time." Each measure has four counts (beats) and each count is the length of a quarter note (♩).

Note and Rest Values in Four Quarter Time:

𝅝   Whole Note: One note played for four counts.

𝅗𝅥   Half Note: Played for two counts.

♩   Quarter Note: Played for one count.

♫   Eighth Notes: Two notes in each count.

▬   Whole Rest: Rest for four counts.

▬   Half Rest: Rest for two counts.

𝄽   Quarter Rest: Rest for one count.

𝄾   Eighth Rest: Rest for a half count.

17. PLAYING ON THE A AND D STRINGS

NEW NOTES: D & A

18. PLAYING ON THE D AND G STRINGS

NEW NOTE: G

19. GOLDFISH

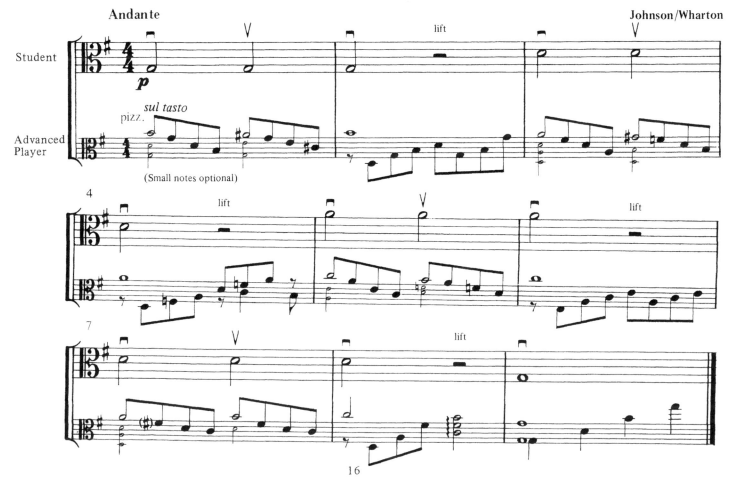

20. OLIVIA'S SONG

2/4 This is the signature for "two quarter time." Each measure has two counts, each the length of a quarter note.

21. A LITTLE RAGTIME

22. HIGHLANDERS

Johnson/Wharton

23. LOWLANDERS

NEW NOTE: C

Johnson/Wharton

24. PLAYING ON TWO STRINGS

25. DOUBLE NOTES

26. DIADS II

27. THE OLD FIDDLER

28. TWO BY TWO

29. FIFTHS

THE REPEAT SIGN: Two dots just before a double bar (in the 2nd and 3rd spaces) indicate that the music coming before this sign is to be repeated. A first ending (⌐1̅⌐) is taken the first time through, and a second ending (⌐2.̅⌐) is substituted for the first ending during the repetition.

30. SUPERSLEUTH

Allegretto

Wharton

*Eighth notes are counted by adding the word "and" between the counts: "1 and 2 and 3 and 4 and 1 and (etc.)".

ACTION 11

LOCATING THE HAND IN FIRST POSITION

PLACING THE FIRST, SECOND AND THIRD FINGERS

Preparation

The fingernails must be kept short at all times. Place the third finger on its signal dot. Make sure the pitch matches the open string to the left which sounds an octave lower. Tap the neck with the thumb and move it back and forth to find its most comfortable position.

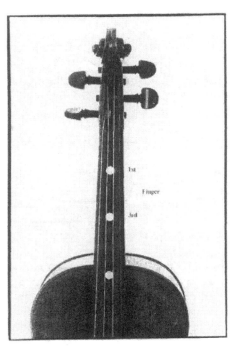

1. Curve the fingers just above the open strings and pluck the D String. (Later perform on all strings.)

2. Drop the first finger to its signal dot.

3. Drop the second finger close to the first. Strike the string with just enough force to produce a good ringing sound.

4. Slide the second finger up a half step to its high position. In its high position, the finger is not as steeply bent.

5. Drop the third finger close to the high second finger. Again, match the pitch with the open string to the left. The fingers must not touch the open string to the right, which must be free to vibrate.

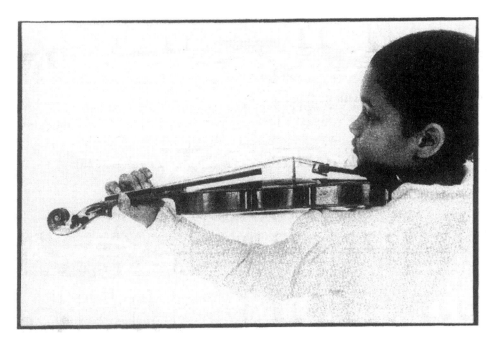

Correct placement of three fingers in the first position.
Place finger tips on the string. Fingernails must be cut short!

31. LOCATING THE HAND IN FIRST POSITION

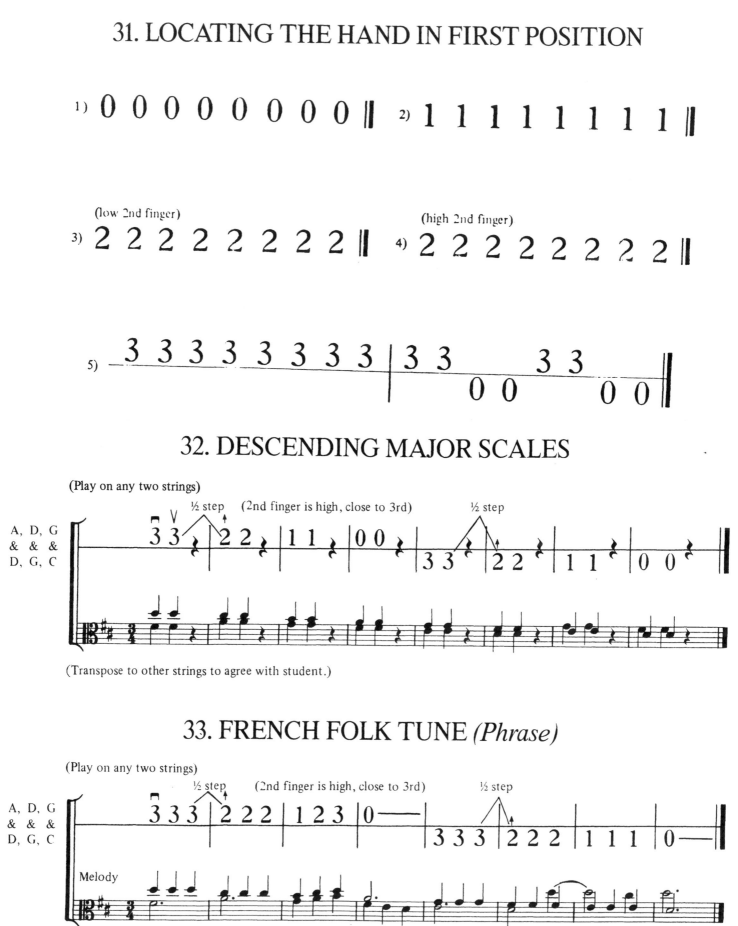

32. DESCENDING MAJOR SCALES

(Play on any two strings)

(Transpose to other strings to agree with student.)

33. FRENCH FOLK TUNE *(Phrase)*

(Play on any two strings)

*The arrow pointing up is a reminder that the 2nd finger is in its high position.

34, a, b & d. VARIATIONS ON AN AIR OF GLUCK *(Phrase)*
(In D, G & C Major)

34c. VARIATIONS ON AN AIR OF GLUCK *(Phrase)*
(In A Major)

35. HOT CROSS BUNS

36. BURNT HOT CROSS BUNS
(Low 2nd Finger)

Play on all strings

Arr. Rolland

37. AU CLAIR DE LA LUNE *(Phrase)*
(High 2nd Finger)

Play on all strings

Au Clair de la lu - ne, Mon a - mi Pier - rot.

Prê - te - moi ta plu - me, Pour é - crire un mot.

38. MARY HAD A LITTLE LAMB

Play on all strings

Mar - y had a lit - tle lamb, lit - tle lamb, lit - tle lamb.

Mar - y had a lit - tle lamb its fleece was white as snow.

*The arrow pointing down is a reminder that the 2nd finger is in its low position.

24

39. TWINKLE, TWINKLE LITTLE STAR

(Play on any two strings)

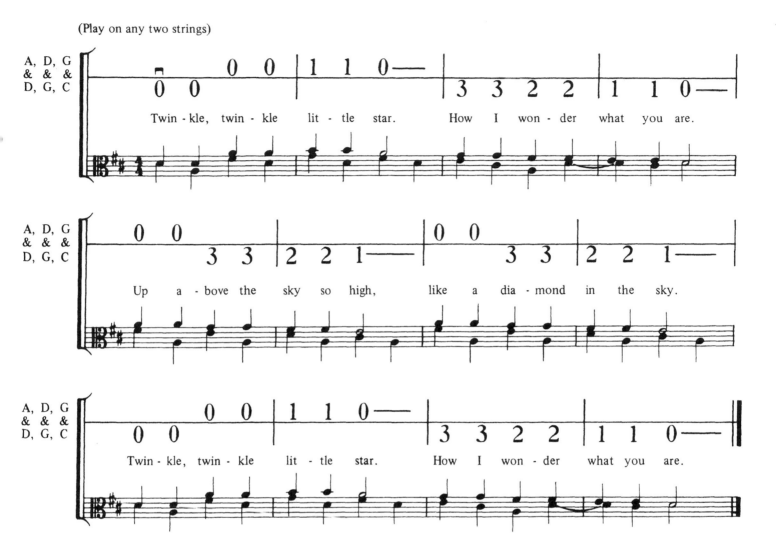

40. MAJOR SCALES

(Play on any two strings)
Play each note four times

41. OLD MACDONALD HAD A FARM *(Phrase)*

(Play on any two strings)

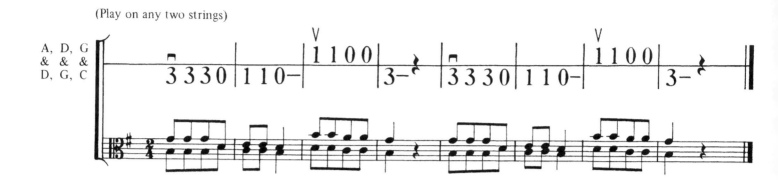

42. LET US CHASE THE SQUIRREL

(Play on any two strings)

Traditional

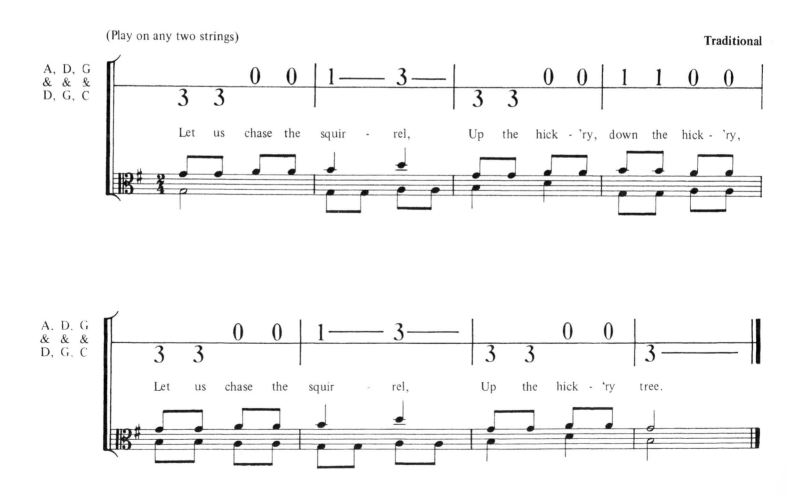

Let us chase the squir - rel, Up the hick - 'ry, down the hick - 'ry,

Let us chase the squir - rel, Up the hick - 'ry tree.

43. JINGLE BELLS

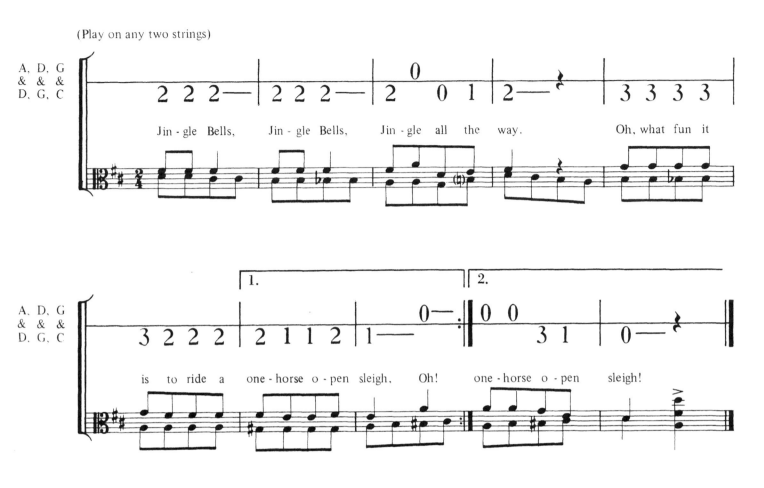

NOTE-READING: PLAYING FIRST FINGER

44. PLAYING FIRST FINGER ON THE A STRING

NEW NOTE: B

45. PLAYING FIRST FINGER ON THE D STRING

NEW NOTE: E

46. PLAYING FIRST FINGER ON THE G STRING

NEW NOTE: A

47. PLAYING FIRST FINGER ON THE E STRING
Tacet

48. PLAYING FIRST FINGER ON THE C STRING

NEW NOTE: D

49. PLAYING FIRST FINGER ON THE D AND G STRINGS

50. PLAYING FIRST FINGER ON THE A AND D STRINGS

The SLUR – indicates that two or more notes are to be played with one bow stroke.

51. CHINESE LULLABY

Rolland

pizz.

sim.

52. GRUMBLING

Rolland

ACTION 12
53. SLURRED STRING CROSSINGS

A.

Go-ing my way

B.

Invent word rhythms

C.

D.

sim.

ACTION 13
PLAYING THE OCTAVE

54. THE OCTAVE GAME

(Play on any two strings)

(Play accompaniments on the same strings the student is playing.)

55. OCTAVE EXERCISE

(Play on any two strings)

56. PONY RIDE

Wharton

(Play on any two strings)

NOTE-READING: PLAYING SECOND FINGER
The Key of A Major (Three Sharps)

57. HOT CROSS BUNS

NEW NOTE: C#

58. THREE NOTE MELODY

Johnson

59. NIMBLE FINGERS

Johnson

The Key of D Major (Two Sharps)

60. HOT CROSS BUNS

61. THREE NOTE MELODY

Johnson

62. NIMBLE FINGERS

Johnson

The Key of G Major (One Sharp)

63. HOT CROSS BUNS

64. THREE NOTE MELODY

Johnson

65. NIMBLE FINGERS

Johnson

The Key of E Major (Four Sharps)
66. HOT CROSS BUNS

67. THREE NOTE MELODY

Johnson

68. NIMBLE FINGERS

Johnson

The Key of C Major (No Sharps or Flats)
69. HOT CROSS BUNS

NEW NOTE: E

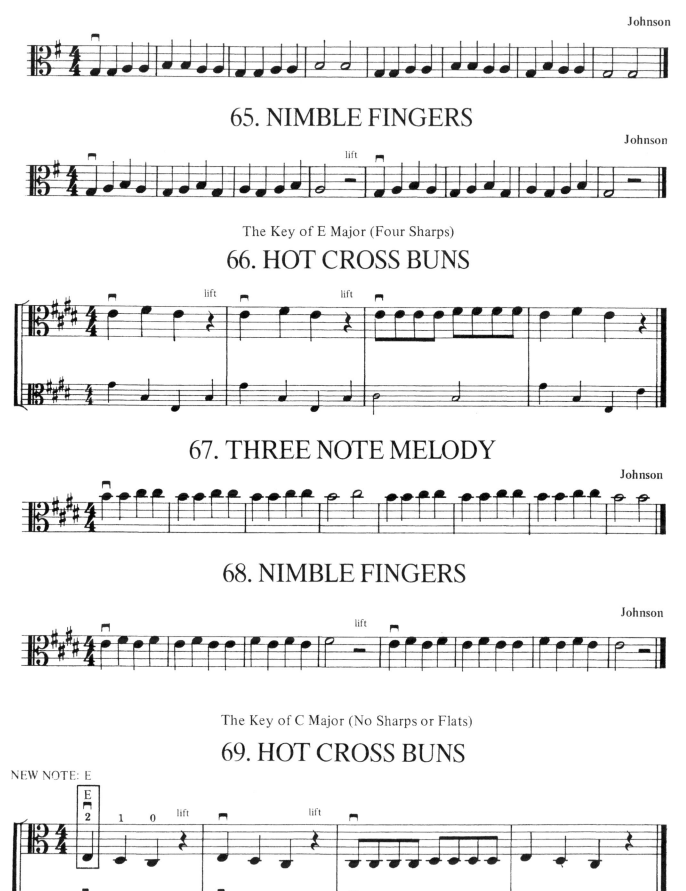

70. THREE NOTE MELODY

Johnson

71. NIMBLE FINGERS

Johnson

This is the signature for "three quarter time." Each measure has three counts, each the length of a quarter note. A dot after a note is called an "augmentation dot." It indicates that the note is played for half again its normal duration. A dotted half note ♩· is held for three counts.

72. MERRY-GO-ROUND
(In D Major)

Johnson

73. MERRY-GO-ROUND
(In A Major)

Johnson

74. MERRY-GO-ROUND
(In G Major)

Johnson

75. MERRY-GO-ROUND
(In C Major)

Johnson

76. DANCE JOSEY

Traditional

77. ROCKY MOUNTAIN

Traditional

ACTION 14
EXTENDING THE BOW STROKE

This action may be performed to the accompaniment of gently lilting music such as *Sweet Little Buttercup.*

Preparation: The *Flying Pizzicato:*

Students extend the arms forward for spacious and free arched pizzicato movements.

1.

2.

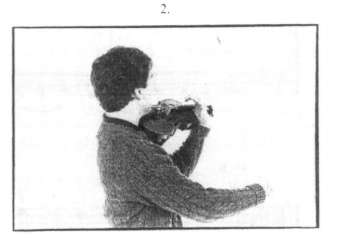

3.

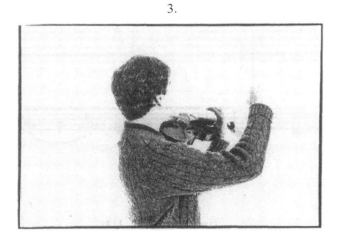

4.

GLOSSARY OF BOWING TERMS:

W.B.	=	Whole bow (Play using the whole bow.)
U.H.	=	Upper half (Play in the upper half of the bow, between the middle and the tip.)
L.H.	=	Lower half (Play in the lower half of the bow, between the frog and the middle.)
Tip	=	Play near the tip.
Frog	=	Play near the frog.

78. WHO'S THAT TAPPING AT THE WINDOW

Traditional
Arr. Wharton

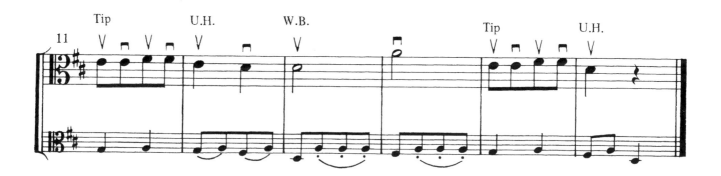

79. EXPLORING D MAJOR

80. DESCENDING D MAJOR SCALE

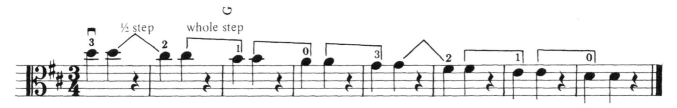

81. D MAJOR SCALE

82. SKIPPING FINGERS AND CROSSING STRINGS
(In D Major)

Johnson

*The line indicates that the finger is to be held down.

83. FRENCH FOLK TUNE

*To sustain the dotted half notes, the speed of the bow must be decreased. To compensate for this, the pressure exerted on the bow stick by the first finger must be slightly increased.

84. JINGLE BELLS

The "up beat" is the last count in each measure. Pieces often start with an up beat, a single note preceding the first full measure. Up beats are usually played up-bow.

85. THE BLUE BELLS OF SCOTLAND

The dotted quarter note (♩.) is held for one and a half counts.

86. THE FARMER IN THE DELL ISN'T WELL

Wharton

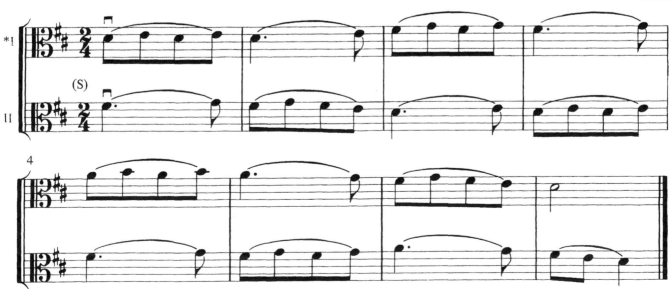

*Practice both part I and part II and play as a duet with teacher or other student, exchanging parts.

39

87. THE FIRST NOWELL

*During the first eleven measures of this piece, the up-bows are twice as fast as the down-bows. To compensate for this increase in speed, the right hand "lifts" the bow gently during its up-stroke to relieve pressure.

88. EXPLORING G MAJOR

89. DESCENDING G MAJOR SCALE

90. G MAJOR SCALE

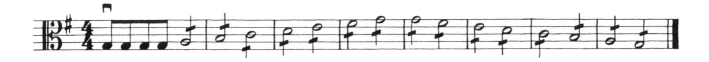

91. SKIPPING FINGERS AND CROSSING STRINGS
(In G Major)

Johnson

92. OLD MACDONALD HAD A FARM

*(S) indicates that the duet accompaniment can be played by the student.

93. THE BLUE BELLS OF SCOTLAND *(Phrase)*
(In G Major)

94. EXPLORING A MAJOR

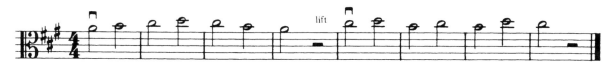

95. DESCENDING A MAJOR SCALE

96. A MAJOR SCALE

97. SKIPPING FINGERS AND CROSSING STRINGS
Tacet

98. THE BLUE BELLS OF SCOTLAND *(Phrase)*
(In A Major)

99. EXPLORING C MAJOR

NEW NOTE: F

100. DESCENDING C MAJOR SCALE

101. C MAJOR SCALE

102. SKIPPING FINGERS AND CROSSING STRINGS
(In C Major)

Johnson

103. THE BLUE BELLS OF SCOTLAND *(Phrase)*
(In C Major)

ACTION 15: REFINING THE BOW STROKE

Practice silent bow placement and transfer, using portions of the bow between:
a.) frog and middle, b.) middle and tip, and c.) frog and tip.

c) FROG-TIP

b) MIDDLE-TIP

a) MIDDLE FROG

NOTE-READING: PLAYING LOW SECOND FINGER

104. BURNT HOT CROSS BUNS
(In A minor)

NEW NOTE: C

Arr. Rolland

lift   lift

105. BURNT HOT CROSS BUNS
(In D minor)

NEW NOTE: F

Arr. Rolland

106. SAMURAI SONG
(In A minor)

Wharton

107. BURNT HOT CROSS BUNS
(In G minor)

NEW NOTE:

Arr. Rolland

108. SAMURAI SONG
(In D minor)

Wharton

109. BURNT HOT CROSS BUNS
Tacet

110. SAMURAI SONG
(In E minor)

Wharton

111. BURNT HOT CROSS BUNS
(In C minor)

Arr. Rolland

NEW NOTE: E♭

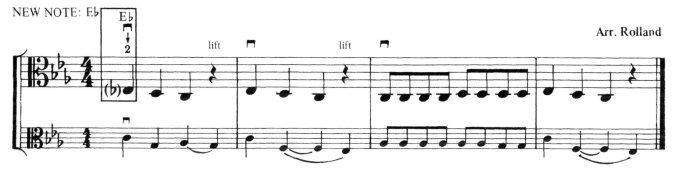

112. SAMURAI SONG
(In G minor)

Wharton

ACTION 16
PLACE AND LIFT THE BOW SILENTLY

Place the bow on the string, fingers curved. Lift the bow as shown, moving the whole arm and bow together. The arm is light!

ACTION 17
SINGLE LIFTED STROKES WITH RETURN (Early Rebound Stroke)

Place the bow gently on the string between the frog and the middle. Draw the bow, curve and lift, and return to the string in a circular movement. Start with short strokes at first, gradually increasing the length of the strokes.

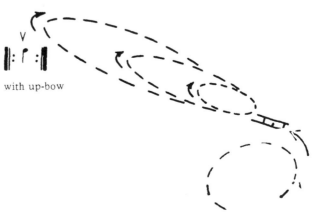

with up-bow

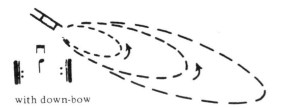

with down-bow

113. EXERCISES FOR SINGLE LIFTED STROKES

Practice these exercises at the frog and at the tip of the bow.

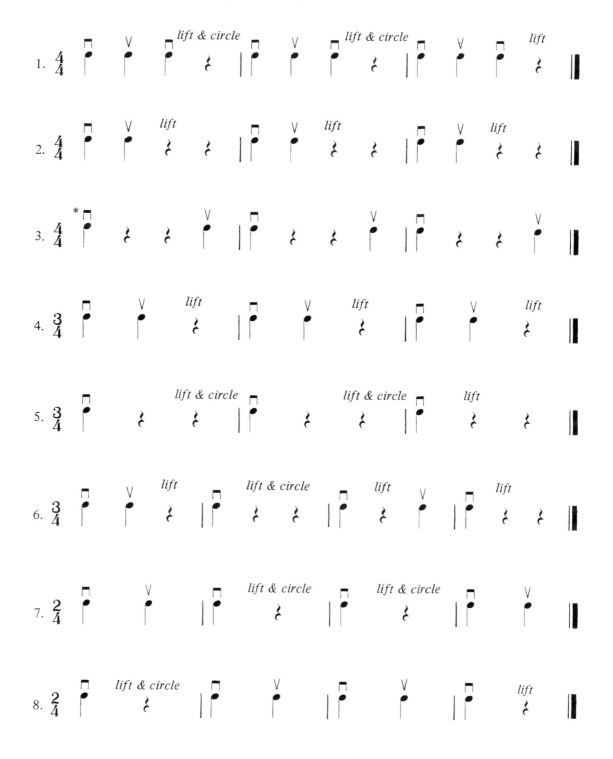

*   The bow is not lifted in this exercise. However the motion is continuous, a follow-through movement when pausing at the tip of the bow making an arch-like movement with the right hand.

114. EXPLORING G MAJOR

115. G MAJOR SCALE

116. THEME FROM BEETHOVEN'S 9TH SYMPHONY
(In G Major)

117. GO TELL AUNT RHODY
(In G Major)

118. EXPLORING C MAJOR

119. C MAJOR SCALE

120. THEME FROM BEETHOVEN'S 9TH SYMPHONY
(In C Major)

121. GO TELL AUNT RHODY
(In C Major)

122. EXPLORING D MAJOR

123. THEME FROM BEETHOVEN'S 9TH SYMPHONY
(In D Major)

124. GO TELL AUNT RHODY
(In D Major)

125. EXPLORING F MAJOR

126. F MAJOR SCALE

127. THEME FROM BEETHOVEN'S 9TH SYMPHONY
(In F Major)

128. GO TELL AUNT RHODY
(In F Major)

NOTE-READING: ALTERNATING HIGH AND LOW SECOND FINGER

129. MAJOR-MINOR
(In A)

Johnson

130. HALF-STEP MARCH
(In A)

Johnson

131. MAJOR-MINOR
(In D)

Johnson

132. HALF-STEP MARCH
(In D)

Johnson

133. MAJOR-MINOR
(In G)

Johnson

134. HALF-STEP MARCH
(In G)

Johnson

135. MAJOR-MINOR
Tacet
136. HALF-STEP MARCH
(In E)

Johnson

137. MAJOR-MINOR
(In C)

Johnson

138. HALF-STEP MARCH
(In C)

Johnson

ACTION 18: LONG SLURRED STROKES

Cross from string to string with a gently curving motion, always approaching a new string level. Raise and lower the arm gradually when approaching the new string. Avoid hasty, jerking movements.

Play these exercises using the Regular Bow Hold.

139. SLURRED STRING CROSSINGS

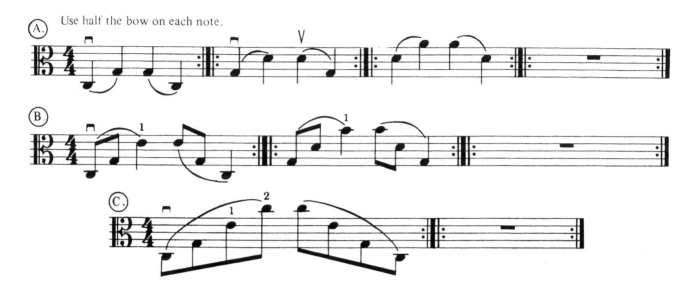

NOTE-READING:

ALTERNATING HIGH AND LOW SECOND FINGER ON NEIGHBORING STRINGS

140. EXPLORING G MAJOR

141. G MAJOR SCALE

142. GOOD KING WENCESLAUS

(S) Melody

(S) Bass

143. SHE'LL BE COMIN' ROUND THE MOUNTAIN
WHEN SHE COMES

(S)

* + = left hand *pizzicato* (pizz.)
Strum all four open strings with the left pinkie.

144. CANON
(In G Major)

THOMAS TALLIS
(1505–1585)

(S)Melody(in canon)

(S) Bass

145. SKIP TO MY LOU
(In G Major)

lift   lift   lift

146. CUCKOO CLOCK
(In G Major)

Wharton

(S)

147. EXPLORING C MAJOR

½ step

148. C MAJOR SCALE

149. CANON
(In C Major)

TALLIS

150. SKIP TO MY LOU
(In C Major)

151. CUCKOO CLOCK
(In C Major)

Wharton

152. EXPLORING D MAJOR

153. D MAJOR SCALE

154. CANON
(In D Major)

TALLIS

Melody (in canon)

Bass

155. SKIP TO MY LOU
(In D Major)

156. CUCKOO CLOCK
(In D Major)

Wharton

157. EXPLORING F MAJOR

158. F MAJOR SCALE

159. CANON
(In F Major)

TALLIS

160. SKIP TO MY LOU
(In F Major)

161. CUCKOO CLOCK
(In F Major)

Wharton

162. CANON IN TWO PARTS

THOMAS TALLIS
(1505—1585)

61

163. STOPPING TWO STRINGS WITH ONE FINGER
(In D Major)

Wharton

*The brackets indicate that one finger (1st, 2nd, or 3rd) is to hold down two strings.

164. STOPPING TWO STRINGS WITH ONE FINGER
(In G Major)

Wharton

165. STOPPING TWO STRINGS WITH ONE FINGER
(In A Major)

Wharton

166. STOPPING TWO STRINGS WITH ONE FINGER
(In C Major)

Wharton

167. ARIA

GEORG PHILIPP TELEMANN
(1681–1767)

"Staccato dot" (•) : Notes are short and separated.

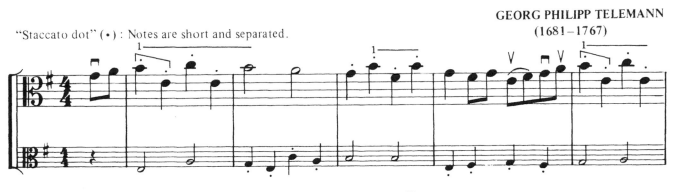

TRIADS AND PENTACHORDS

168. D MAJOR

169. D MINOR

170. G MAJOR

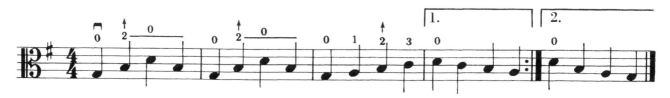

171. G MINOR

172. A MAJOR

173. A MINOR

174. C MAJOR

175. C MINOR